The Exorcist Head Turn Effect

How to write headlines that turn heads like a demon possessed girl and command attention to make rivers of revenue

By Albert Noguera

Introduction

Hello! This is Albert Noguera, email copywriter extraordinaire. Welcome to "The Exorcist Head Turn Effect."

Thank you for investing in yourself and snagging up a copy of this book.

You know what that means...?

RESULTS ARE RIGHT AROUND THE CORNER.

That deserves a pat on the back. I want you to go to a mirror and praise yourself. Go ahead, I'll wait...

Ok. Now that you're back.

In this short book, I'll teach you how to write headlines that captures the attention of your audience.

You're going to learn a big part of a proven system businesses have used to double their profits.

You lucky devil.

Here's what this book is NOT about:

I won't be covering how to write sales letters.

Or video scripts.

Or facebook posts.

But these principles will make writing all that 10 times more effective.

These principles aren't just for emails, they are adaptable. You can use them for podcasts, videos, blog posts, articles, instagram caption, and of course books.

Why would you want to adapt anyway?

Attention!

In today's world, there's so much noise that you have to learn to break through all that noise.

Even if you had the best copywriters and marketers in the world on your team, it doesn't mean a thing if you don't have the end consumers attention.

This makes it possible.

The legendary John Caples said, "A headline is worth 50% of the selling power of a sales letter."

Don't worry if you've never done this before.

If I can do it, you can too.

This isn't rocket science. It's just science.

And once you learn the science, add a dab of passion, sprinkle in some fun...

BOOM!

You got the perfect combination to make your customers go into a piranha buying fury.

Unfortunately, that's only half the battle.

There's also the body copy part. Once the reader is in, now what?

Wait?

Whaaat?

You want me to talk about that too?

Geez, why so needy? Fine. I'll do it.

Well, this book is about attention capturing headlines but the other is important too.

So I'll briefly touch on it. But only because I like you.

And I also believe in over delivering whenever I can.

All right, let's get this party started!

Part 1: Breaking Down An Exorcist Head Turning Headline

This is the first thing your readers are going to see.

So it's your chance to make a good first impression. And make no mistake, first impressions matter.

You want a headline that commands the attention of your reader like a beautiful blonde in a tight black dress walking through a construction yard.

Why?

Because, attention is the currency of today's modern business world. If you don't have attention, you don't have a business.

Accomplished copywriter and brilliant marketer, Doberman Dan calls it the "Rack The Shotgun" effect.

One night, Doberman Dan was woken up in the middle of the night by a strange man standing next to his bed where him and his wife were sleeping.

He quickly reached under his bed, pulled out his 12 gauge, pointed it at the bad guy and racked it in his face.

How's that for capturing attention?

The good news for you is that most people don't do this. Or even know about it.

So that's where you can have a competitive advantage.

By using a Exorcist Head Turning Headline.

Something so attention-stopping like witnessing a demon possessed girl completely turning her head around.

Hopefully, your reader isn't possessed, that would lower conversions.

A good headline is composed of these principles:

- Surprise!!
- Curiosity
- Benefit
- Bizarre
- Popular phrases and quotes
- Contrast
- Book and movie titles
- Famous characters
- Numbers and lists
- Mingling time

We will get to these in a moment but first we have get rid of your bad programming.

7 Reasons Why Most Headlines Stink Like Hairy Monkey Balls

1) Blase' Headlines

These are headlines that cause zero emotion.

For example, "3 Billion People Use The Internet On A Daily Basis."

When I read that, I think:

And...?

You're just stating a fact. Nobody cares about facts. People want to be entertained.

You want to stir up emotions in your reader.

Look, I get it. I've made this mistake before too. I knew the product too well and it made me too invested.

I cared too much!

So you've got to take a step back and write from a place of ease. And then enter the conversation in their mind.

That's when you get headlines like this:

"How Trolling Your Customers Like President Trump Can Double Your Income"

Instead of this lame one, "70% Of Internet Use Is Done From A Phone"

See the difference?

One is boring and the other excites the reader to continue reading.

2) Kim Kardashian Diva

Miss Kim K, the social media queen that's famous for being famous. What does she have to do with writing headlines you ask?

If you've ever stumbled upon her instagram or seen her tv show, (Hey, I don't judge) then you've seen her many, many, many, many, many, many, selfies and photos.

Yeah Albert, she likes to take pictures of her big booty, what about it?

It's all EGO!

Everything says me, me, me. I'm not hating though, she's a brilliant marketer. I learn a lot from her as should you. More power to her.

When it comes to you, you're not a world famous reality star. You don't have hundreds of millions of fans worshiping your behind.

But this is exactly what a lot of copywriters do. They make it about themselves.

Hogging the spotlight turns off your reader because it does two things:

First it takes the focus off the reader and makes it about you. No good. Make it about them and their problems and fears.

Second it makes you look douchey. It reminds of that guy Shooter McGavin from the movie Happy Gilmore. No one likes that guy. Don't be that guy.

3) Bugs Bunny Headlines

No I don't mean you can't use cool catchphrases, "Eh...What's up, doc?"

You should model and use them.

What you don't want is fluffy bunny headlines.

Like, "Get in today to start making $300 a day and don't miss out on this limited time opportunity non-scam offer before it ends at midnight tonight."
Too wordy. (And scammy sounding)

Now, there's nothing wrong with a long headline IF every word is impactful. But most headlines have too much fluff and not enough bang.

I recommend the Obvious Adams for this. It's short and will get you to think about how you can be as direct as possible with your headlines.

4) Being Too Vague

If you asked me how I would improve your business with ema ls. And I said I would write emails.

Would that satisfy you?

That's what I thought. So why do it in your headlines?

Vague promises are everywhere now-a-days.

"Get more girls" "Make money online" "Step ya game up son"

You know what's crazy?

These headlines worked hundreds of years ago. Especially that last one. Entrepreneurs during Lincoln's time were all about "son" and "stepping game up." They were the first rappers. I swear.

But seriously, a headline like, "Lose Fat" worked insanely good back then and made a ton of sales.

Today is different.

With today's ever shortening attention span thanks to instagram and facebook, you've got to be more clever with your headlines.

5) Mysterious Stranger

Old skool copywriters will hate me for saying this but curiosity ain't all it's cut out to be.

There was a famous copywriter and marketer named Gary Halbert.

If you don't know him, depending on who you ask he was Michael Jordan, Kobe Bryant or Lebron James of the copywriting world.

So basically one of the very best to ever do it.
One day Gary was out on the water in his boat with his friend. This is where he went to go think of new ideas for his business. His friend was also a copywriter.

Gary asked him, "What do you think is the most important appeal in marketing is?" His friend said, "That's easy, it's self-interest"

Gary corrected him, "Wrong. It's curiosity."

Now, I'm not saying not to use curiosity. You abso-toot-ly should. But if it's a curiosity-only headline, not good.

When you do that the reader may get confused because it's too vague.

See, your headline should be worth remembering and solid.

Curiosity-only headlines leaves the reader to fend for himself or herself. You're leaving it up to them to make sense of it. You're playing charades but your acting skills suck.

Bottom line is vagueness is the death of conversions.

6) Put A Ring On It

Lacking a promise or benefit will doom you to the graveyard of copywriting hell.

"How To Blow $9.2 Billion And Then Become The Most Powerful Man In The World"

If Trump wrote another book, this could be the title. What an attention grabber!

The headline hints at losing at an extreme level and then coming back and literally going all the way to the tippy top of success.

You've got to spark a fire within your reader and make them want to drop what they're doing and read your stuff.

In the words of Queen B: "If you liked it, then you should have put a ring on it
Don't be mad once you see that he want it"

And that's exactly what'll happen if you don't use benefits and promises. Some other dude is gonna come along and snatch your girl up.

So don't be cheap. Get her that phat diamond ring.

She's worth it. I promise.

7) Don't Be A Debbie Downer

You know that one friend that's never invited but shows up anyways and everybody avoids them...and if you don't know who it is, it's you.

Just kidding.

Maybe.

Possibly.

Anyhoo, the reason everyone ignores that friend is because they are negative clouds of energy. It feels icky to be around them.

Now think about the guy that everyone loves to be around. The total opposite.

He's charismatic, fun to hang out with, funny, and generally just good vibes radiate off him. That's how you want your headline to come off.

The reader should feel like this is a ship that can sail them into the land of their dreams.

Paint the vision.

Speak the positive language that's already inside their head and focus on that.

For example: Don't focus on all your friends making more money than you while you're broke. Focus on everybody jealously staring at you like you're a walking million dollar sign when you've made it.

By the way, you can only do this if you have an intimate understanding of your market. You must use empathy to come up with winning headlines.

Got it?

Good

With those copywriting sins out of the way, on to the good stuff...

Part 2: 10 Secrets To Write Headlines That Work So Good Customers Can't Look Away

I must give credit where credit is due to my email mentor Ben Settle. When it comes to email, he is a godsend.

This guy knows his stuff! You can find him at www.bensettle.com.

If you want to really develop your skill with email, this is the guy to learn from. He sells a monthly newsletter called Email Players.

It teaches you the fundamentals of email. Very expensive but very worth it if you're a serious student of email copywriting.

I highly recommend him. He no longer does any client work so if you're looking to hire, you're s.o.l. (shit outta luck).

Fortunately, I do client work. But I can't help everybody because my time is limited and I can only work with a handful of businesses that meet a strict (but reasonable) criteria.

Apply here: http://albertnoguera.com/apply

Onward:

Here we are, the point where we go over writing headlines for emails, also known as subject lines.

The subject line and the overall theme of your email is the second most important part as far as getting it read.

What's the most important? Your name.

When subscribers see the "from" name, it makes all the difference. But I can't help you there because this book is about headlines.

And that is something I can help you with.

Ideally I like to start with a writing a subject line first and then the body copy.

Sometimes I get an idea for the message I want to talk about first and I just write it. Then I tie in the subject line around it.

Whatever floats your boat is fine. As long you follow these 10 principles, you'll win.

Consider me Moses, the shepherd.

You're my people, the lamb.

Now follow me and I'll lead you to the promised land...

1) Surprise 'em

First of all this is very effective but two things:
- One, don't use this technique in every email
- Two, don't just use it for the sake of using it

If you use this subject line, you've got to have a strategy behind it. If you don't, you're going to rub people the wrong way and bad things shall come.

You'll lose subscribers and lower your conversions.

Don't say I didn't warn ya.

And remember, you don't have to use this tactic at all. You can just use the other 12.

So what is it?

It's just like it says - surprise 'em. Shock the hell out of them actually.

The entire goal of this type of this subject line is to get people to open up your email and read it.

It's a way of shaking people out of their normal routine. Most people are in a state of apathy and life has become routine. This wakes them up.

You want your copy to give the reader a mini adventure and this type of subject line does that. It's just a short little adventure.

But you have to pay if off quickly in the email. Don't drag it out and make the reader wait for the punchline.

No need to be a jerk.

Because, if you do make them wait, you'll likely annoy them and make them think you're just crude.

So again, I stress to use your better judgement when creating this shock effect type headline.

Here are some examples:

Give it to me bad boy

He couldn't stop himself from coming

You have cancer

How to S.H.I.T. on your customers

2) Curious about how to build curiosity

As Gary Halbert said, curiosity is the greatest weapon for a copywriter. It's the prime force in getting your emails read.

It works so good that people will sometimes be reading a 27 page sales letter and a bullet point infused with mind-teasing curiosity got them to buy a very expensive product.

Master this and you'll find your open rates skyrocket like Elon Musk's BFR (Big F**king Rocket).

And that's never a bad thing.

More people consuming your content usually means more sales.

Curiosity is titillating. (I like that word, titillating)

It's the w-40 greased slide between your prospect and your product. And there's no better grease than curiosity.

People are smashed with ad after ad after ad every single day. You have to break through if you even want a chance.

Generating curiosity will help you do that.

There are several ways to create curiosity. You can use an oxymoron or two conflicting ideas.

It could be an accident. Like someone accidentally finding diamonds in their backyard.

Curiosity creates an itch in your reader and if you do it right by combining it with the other principles, they can't just leave and forget about it.

It's an itch that they just have to scratch.

Some examples:

How to use violence to turn your haters into dollars

What never to tell your wife in bed

The lazy way to riches

A dead "giveaway" which proves if a guru is lying to you

How to hit your financial "G-spot" and create a flood of sales

There are six deadly sins that could shatter your business...And you're already making four of them!

Four "little target" words that can help you win your lover's heart forever

3) Plain old benefit

Nothing magical here.

Just include or imply a promise or benefit in your headline.

This usually works better for people who already know, like and trust you. So if you're sending cold traffic to a sales page with a benefit-only headline, it might not be the best idea.

You'll do better with curiosity for those prospects.

Depending on your market, what these benefits will be about will change.

That's what you should be thinking about. Who is my market?

What are the right questions you should be asking? Or answering?

What do they care about?

What unfulfilled emotional desires burn within them?

What is is that they truly want?

Join the community so you can figure out what's actually going on inside your market's mind.

Then use it to create your subject line.

Examples:

Weight loss answered

How to create massive revenue with your current customers

How to add an extra $200,000 to your business with just 4 emails

How to master your jump shot like Steph Curry

The one best way to win the true undying love of a member of the opposite sex

4) Phrases and quotes

Recently Conor Mcgregor has gotten a lot of criticism for what he did to a rival group.

He crashed a rival's press conference and then followed him and his team outside to the bus area.

Then Conor picked up some object, I'm not sure what it was, and threw it at the window of the bus.

It shattered.

There were a few fighters near that window and their eyeballs got cut up. They had to drop out of their upcoming fights because of this.

If Conor had thrown this object at the luggage door on the bottom of the bus, a couple of people would have said that he's a badass.

But since he did what he did, the ENTIRE world is talking about him. Some like him more and some like him less.

The point is, he was **hacking culture** whether he knew it or not. He probably did since he's the greatest combination of marketer/fighter I've ever seen.

And playing on popular quotes and phrases is a way to hack culture in your headlines.

By doing this you enter into the mind of the masses. It makes it fun to read and engages them.

And when you engage people in this way, it's very hard for them to look away.

Hacking examples:

It's the people, stupid

Do you understand the words coming out of my copy?

Keep calm and make money

Liberty and sales for all

Love stuck on stupid

Say hello to my marketing genius friend

5) World of weird

Another subject line secret that's sure to rip your customers faces open.

What?

I don't even know what I just said. I've been writing for a while.

Anyway, this is where you tap into your reader's sense of wonder by using a weird or bizarre theme.

There's something in tabloids that gets people to read when it says, "Rihanna sleeps with little aliens from Mars."

It's bizarre...

...But it gets people to open that email up.

Because it's different.

People are used to seeing 450 emails with the same headline that's selling something.

It's the same old same old.

Companies claiming that their thing is the best ever.

It's not new, it's normal.

Just copy and paste over and over.

But always bring your body copy full circle and tie it to this headline.

All it takes is one.

One email that doesn't make sense and pay off in the body copy and you lose that customer forever. They tune you out.

Do it right and you'll open yourself up to more sales.

The bizzaro examples:

Superman smashes weight loss incest

The Exorcist Head Turn Effect (Ayy, that sounds familiar)

Demon portal to marketing madness

The flying dildo of success

Marketers playing with ghosts

Why your fingernails might literally be ruining your bank account

6) Conflicting Ideas

Ooo wee! This one's a goodie.

This is another play on curiosity but in a very specific way...contrast.

Put two opposing thoughts or ideas together and...BOOM...you've got yourself a itch-that-I-just-need-to-scratch of a headline.

Most copywriters that use it don't even know their doing it, from what I can tell. Because, nobody talks about it.

They don't realize how truly potent this technique is.

But now you do.

So go on young padawan, use this for your all your marketing desires, and may the force be with you.

Examples:

The crazy thing is even if you're lazy, it works

How to yell in the library and have everyone love you for it

Attract more customers by giving less value

Hitler's noble marketing secrets

How to pick up a girl by not talking to her

Why going out of business is good for business

7) Harry Potter Incest

You might be thinking, what the heck is this subtitle Albert?

Let me explain...interweave into your headlines book and movie titles.

As you can see, I chose Harry Potter Incest because it's the biggest movie/book combos in the world.

It's also what I grew up on as a millennial.

Speaking of Harry Potter, the billionaire author J.K. Rowling was asked about her thought process when she was writing the books...

...she said "I write for me. I write what I find amusing."

This is what you should be doing also. Write with self-amusement when you create your headlines. And also when you write your body copy.

This is a trick to know if your copy will work or not. Also, It'll come off much more authentic and natural.

More:

So what your doing is just playing around with these titles and adding and subtracting words so they match the theme of your email.

I'm not a legal expert but it's totally legal as far as I know. So don't worry about infringement or anything.

Just don't blatantly copy the title word for word and you'll be fine.

Incesty examples:

The magic of unbelieving

How to win customers and persuade them

Think and grow your sex life

Lead the copywriting field

The money games

The avengers lost health secret

Mr. and Mrs. Copywriter

8) Famous Characters

For some reason people connect with characters from tv and movies.

It's like they have this hypnotic spell over people. Maybe because on some level people wish they were these characters?

I don't know but what I do know is that using this technique in your subject lines will increase your open rates and get you more fat stacks of the green stuff.

Let me stress the word, FAMOUS.

This only works if your market knows who you're referencing.

If it's some character from a long canceled tv show from your childhood, No bueno mi amigo.

They have to get the reference.

Dany, dragons, dating lies

Peter Griffin's Persuasion Secrets

Ellen fights the fat monster

The godfather's unrefusable sales method

Monk's quirky but effective marketing blueprint

Harry and Lloyd's dumb and dumber ways to riches

9) Numbers and Lists

A very powerful (and profitable) way to write headlines.

This is a very easy, beginner friendly way to write emails and subject lines.

You just have to make sure that the overall idea is tied to something that your market cares about.

Do that and this method draws people in like a seductive lover.

Listy examples:

3 ways to make $100 a day as a 15 year old

4 sure-fire ways to tell if your spouse has cheated on you recently

10 biggest secrets to double your income in 30 days

7 foods that will boost your t-levels and spark almost magic-like attraction in the opposite sex

2 simple ways to give your woman mind-blowing-toe-curling orgasms over and over

10) Single and ready to mingle

Have you ever heard of idea sex?

This is when you take two completely different ideas that have nothing to do with each other and put them together. Then out comes a beautiful baby of an idea.

Same thing with this.

Take the previous 9 ways you've learned how to write headlines and make them do each other.

Until you've got yourself a hard, throbbing, irresistible headline.

Combine two or three or more, it doesn't matter.

Over time, as you practice, you'll naturally start doing this without even thinking about it.

Examples:

Jon Snow brawls with instagram gurus...this is famous character, bizarre, popular culture, curiosity.

Kobe Bryant's weird imaginary basketball exercise to make bushels of cash with email...we've got famous character, weird, benefit, curiosity.

7 ways to piss off your customers...we have numbers and lists, contrast, curiosity.

How to ignore your girlfriend and have her LOVE you for it...this is a play on benefit, contrast, curiosity.

Why you should encourage your children to drop out of school if you care about their success...obviously this is using contrast, surprise, benefit, curiosity

Part 3: Let's invade their heads

The body copy...what comes after someone reads and your headline and clicks.

What do you say?

Well, what I'm about to teach you is the most important thing when it comes to copywriting.

This will determine if you make a million dollars or nothing at all.

So make sure to take this seriously and you'll have the secret to marketing success.

Ready.

Set.

Go.

You want to create a character for your market. An avatar.

One character that you can picture in your mind whenever you're writing.

This person will have a name and you'll know everything about them. And I mean every single little detail his or her life.

This character will represent your overall market.

I can stop writing right now and you can take this secret to make boatloads of moola.

Okay, I'll go a little longer.

(Aren't-cha glad you have lil' ole me in your corner?)

Now, it's important to realize that you don't want sell to everybody.

That's how you get tire kickers and freebie seekers onto your list.

Doing this avatar creation exercise will help you to flush out those people from your list. They're never going to buy from you anyway so why would you want them there?

This will leave you with all your dream customers. The ones you WANT to do business with.

When creating this avatar, you want to think and feel from the point of view of your avatar.

- What makes them tick
- What are their needs
- Their issues
- Their pain
- Their deepest desires
- Their aspirations
- Their frustrations
- Their problems
- Their concerns
- Etc

After you've done this exercise, you'll have a far deeper connection with your audience and your copywriting will be much more smooth.

It will be easier and the words will flow out of you.

Here are two tricks to help you:

1) While doing this is, find a picture of your ideal character and give him or her a name.

Look at it while you answer these avatar creation questions. It will bond you to this person and pull out your empathy.

2) After you create your ideal customer avatar. Create a second avatar. Only this time, create an avatar of the ideal person you want to AVOID as a customer.

Answer the same questions for this person and also give them a name and picture.

By having to two avatars, you will have given yourself a massive edge over your competitors because they will never do this.

They will keep spinning their wheels and you'll have the midas touch.

When it comes to writing your body copy, (and headlines) this is like stealing candy from a baby.

You don't need to worry if you said the wrong thing because you know exactly who you're talking to.

It's like talking to your best friend. You don't need to think about what to say. You just say whatever's on your mind because it's your closest friend. You have a deep bond with that person and you know how to speak their language.

Part 4: Alberto's Email Examples

I figured it would help you to see how I mix the subject lines and body copy together.

So you can see how I flow them together.

Below I've given you emails and headlines for different niches and industries to prove to you that these principles you've learned can be applied to almost any market.

It doesn't matter which market you're in because these are evergreen principles that work on humans, not markets.

Markets change, technology changes, governments change, but human nature never changes.

Not for the next 100 years anyway. And by then, you and me will be long gone.

Warning: Do not copy my emails word for word. That's just low man. And second, the offer won't fit your audience. I wrote these call to actions for that audience and that's why they work.

You'd only be scratching the surface of the email's persuasion powers.

But do read them.

Do reread them.

And do learn from them and create your own emails and headlines from the structure and flow. Not the content.

Here's some profit pulling emails that I've strung together for ya, enjoy:

Email #1: In this email I talk about a true story about me and this girl. I brought up curiosity and how it works in both business and with women. In the end I plug my email copywriting services.

How I made her want me even after I called her ugly

This is a weird thing that happened to me recently.

I was surprised as you may have guessed. But there's a lesson you can learn from this, if you want to make money, or even for life in general.

For privacy purposes I'll call her Melanie.

Anyway here's what happened:

Melanie is this girl that's in my social circle that I see sometimes when all our friends hang out. She's been trying to get in yours truly's pants for while now. One day I was talking to her and said, "All the girls here are ugly. No offense though." Of course she said, "Wowww, you just called me ugly."

She didn't talk to me for the rest of that night.

But a funny thing happened the next time I saw her. She asked me out on a date to get sushi! And for my phone number.

Wth!

I thought she was done with me after I said that.

But it turns out that it only made her want me more because no one has ever said that to her in her entire life.

It made her curious.

And curiosity done properly, equals lots of lovin from the ladies.

Well, guess what?

When it comes to making money on the interwebs, curiosity is the key. Once you've set off their curiosity alarm, the human brain can't shut off. It has to find the answer!

If you want to never worry about money ever again, just remember this one secret.

It has created billions of dollars in many, many industries and businesses.

And you know what's even better?

What if someone created an entire email system that had mind-teasing curiosity already embedded in it?

What if you could clone that system and make boatloads of cash?

Better yet, what if you didn't have to do it at all? And, instead had an expert at this system do all the heavy lifting for you?

Would that interest you?

A real game changer that would be. Fortunately, there is such a thing:

http://albertnoguera.com/apply

Albert Noguera

Email #2: This email is a weird one. I wrote it on St. Paddy's day and It's about my childhood and what I saw, (or didn't see) depending on what you believe. I'm promoting a popular clickbank affiliate offer called cb passive income in this one.

Leprechauns are the truth

Today is St. Patrick's day, meant to celebrate the death of St. Patrick of course.

I don't know how leprechauns got involved with this day but whatevs.

Every year on this day, I'm reminded of my childhood of when I lived in an apartment complex called Shamrock. The logo was a clover.

One day I was alone at home and I saw something at the end of the hallway. As I took a closer look, what I saw surprised me:

A leprechaun.

I got super scared and I ran to grab the bat behind the couch.

Being as nervous as I was, I walked up slowly to it and it ran into the kitchen. Once in the kitchen, it sped past me down the hall and into the bathroom. So again I followed it into the bathroom.

But once I got there…

Nothing.

He disappeared.

This magical creature evaded me and I never saw it again.

Since this happened so long ago, I really don't know if it was a lucid dream or for real.

You can decide for yourself.

Point is, this childhood experience reminds me of something else that's green and evades people.

That's right…moolah.

It seems like most people trying to succeed online fail more often than not. And it's not their fault. It's not your fault if this is you.

You can never tell which "gurus" are actually giving you the real deal or just trying to make money off of you.

That's why I'm so glad I found cb passive income.

It's a fully automated system that does 95% of the work for you.

Your only job?

Drive traffic. That's it.

So if you finally want to catch those evasive little green monsters (money not leprechauns), check it out:

[Link]

Albert Noguera

Email #3: I talk about diapers, garl c, and text books in this one. Strange, yes. But in order to get good at email, you have to learn how to connect every day scenarios with your product. Once you learn that, you'll be an email MACHINE.

Diaper and garlic's secret to cheap text books

My sister was making spaghetti and garlic bread for dinner because I was coming to visit her and my new born nephew.

When I got there I could smell that familiar smell of homemade mom's spaghetti. That recipe for the spaghetti? She got it from her mama. (I mean. our mama hehe)

But the garlic bread, a bit overcooked.

Actually it was burnt and I didn't really care to eat it.

She said she was changing little man's diaper and she left the garlic bread in the oven a little too long.

Don't get me wrong, the spaghetti was still good but it would have hit the just the right spot with that garlic bread.

All lost due to stinky poops.

You know what else stinks?

Text books.

The prices anyway.

Some books can go for over $300! What in the world?!

I remember being in college, that was a lot of smackaroos to put up.

Luckily, I have a solution. (as I give an evil grin)

Instead of spending hundreds of dollars on a text book you'll only open a handful of times, you can rent them for a fraction of the cost.

Save up to 85%

Check it out here: [Link]

Albert Noguera

Email #4: This time I'm promoting a real estate program that teaches people how to buy and flip house quickly and I tie it in with a story of me eating mozzarella cheese sticks. Btw, those things are sooo goood, mmmmm.

Why mozzarella sticks can make you a full time income with part time work

You might get a kick out of this.

Last week, I was at a local Italian restaurant with a friend. We ordered mozzarella cheese sticks as appetizers because you can never go wrong with those.

When I put that stick in my mouth, instantly it confirmed what I suspected, these cheese sticks were absolutely delicious.

I couldn't stop.

I was scarfing down those things like my life depended on it and pretty soon....my belly was full. How was I going to fit the rest of the main dish!?

And you know what?

This reminded me of the flipping real estate game.

You don't have to invest for a full 30 years to make money, you can take the appetizer approach.

Which is flipping real estate. (and doesn't take a lot of time)

It's simple.

You buy a foreclosed house, give it a little TLC, and sell it.

Enter The Real Estate Investing Program
It can help you accomplish all the things we discussed.

Here's the link: www.udemy.com/discover-how-to-fix-and-flip-houses-step-by-step/

Albert Noguera

Email #5: In this email, I promote a digital dating product called 77 ways to make her want to f.u. Watch my opening, I use one word and talk about that one word and then apply it to selling the product.

The whacky crazy 77 ways to make women want you

A couple weeks back while I was reading a book called "Just Sell The Damn Thing" by Dan Doberman, I stumbled across this word.

Titillating.

I like that word. It amuses me.

Google tells me that the definition is: arousing mild sexual excitement or interest.

Nice.

I could think of a few people who could use a word like this.

They couldn't titillate a woman even if she handed it to him on a silver platter.

Some guys don't even know where to begin.

But guess what?

All is not lost.

Jason Capital's 77 ways to make her want to f.u. is here

In it, is all the titillation you'll ever need.

And, the best part?

You don't need all 77. You only need to master 3 ways and you're set for life.

Operation Titillate starts now: [Link]
Albert Noguera

Email#6: Obscurity equals business death. Being number one in google is what a lot of people want. I talk about how to rank on the first page and dominate the search engines.

Be the google cheetah by chasing away the competition and eating them whole

While watching a documentary on the wild animals of our world, there was a segment about cheetahs.

The cheetah is the fastest animal on land. They can reach speeds up to 70 mph.

Whoo!

Once they set their eyes on you, it's pretty much over. You can't escape.

This cheetah was chasing down her prey, a gazelle.

The gazelle tried to run but after just a few seconds, the wild cat jumped and captured its prey in one fell swoop.

And you want to know something?

That example of nature at its purest isn't so different from the world of search engines and google.

What difference would it make if you could chase your competition off the top ranking spots in google and placed yourself there?

Not only once but multiple times?

You'd eat up the competition.

If you're ready to be the cheetah and stop being the prey, go here: [Link]

Albert Noguera

Email #7: I tell a story of me working out and almost destrcying my foot to self-improvement. How it relates and what the similarities are.

Improve yourself by smashing your foot

Health is a big factor for success.

If you don't have your health, you don't have anything. So I hit the gym 3-4 times a week to maintain and improve my health.

One day I was doing squats with some heavy weight.

After I finished my set I clumsily dropped the plate.

I mean, it was ONLY INCHES away!

Picture wearing soft nike shoes, no steel toe protection and a 100lb piece of solid metal crashing down on your foot.

Yeah I got lucky.

But as the saying goes, the show must go on.

And that's exactly what I did. I endured the pain and finished my workout.

Just like physical exercise is good for your health. Self-improvement is good for your mind.

You may face some unexpected bumps in the road but if you keep at it you'll end up a better version of yourself in the end.

The good thing is, you won't have to worry about demon weights trying to maim you.

To start building your six pack of the mind,

Go here: [Link]

Albert Noguera

Email #8: People are more motivated to avoid pain than to gain pleasure. It's just human nature. Knowing this, I used fear to create a desire for my product, life insurance.

Freeze a snowman of death

What do you call a snowman in the summer?

A puddle

I know...lame

But there's also truth in it.

Just like a snowman can be kicked down by a rebel child or melted down to a puddle by the scorching sun, your life is just as fragile.

Imagine going out to eat with your family on a Sunday afternoon and all of a sudden...you feel it.

You can't breathe.

It feels like an elephant is standing on your chest.

Your left arm goes numb.

You hear your spouse scream in terror.

The room starts to fade to black...

A heart attack.

Just like that, you no longer walk this earth and you leave your family to handle the awful burden.

Something that they're not prepared for. (Most people aren't)

But what if you could protect your family?

What if you could leave them with $250,000 in the event that you kick the bucket.

Well, I've got good news and bad news.

First the bad news, you've got to pass on for them to receive the benefits.

The good news is that you can get started today and have the peace of mind to know that your family will be taken care of if anything happens to you.

And the crazy part?

You can get started for only $14 a month!

Here's the link: [Link]

Albert Noguera

Email #9: Most people love getting a discount on anything they can. This email invites them to do just that by signing up and using ebates, a cashback website, for their tummy needs. I also start with a story about flat tires and tie it into the offer.

Why I don't do grocery stores

Have you ever been excited to do something and then something unexpected happens and ruins it?

Speeding down the freeway, on my way to a bbq at a friend's house and then...I heard it...

a loud POP!

Burning rubber filled my nose.

The speedometer started to fall and fall no matter how hard I pushed the gas pedal.

I pulled over to the shoulder and inspected the damage, the entire left rear tire had been destroyed. Never has there been a flatter tire in existence. (I checked)

Anyway, here's why I told you that story:

Many people overspend on groceries and eating out than they realize.

And thus, leaving their bank account as flat as that tire.

Living on a dime has a new e-course that can help you cut your grocery bill as much as 50%!

One satisfied customer said she saved over $10,000 after applying what she learned in the program.

Don't let your bank account flatten ever again:

[Link]

Albert Noguera

Email #10: Who doesn't love food? It's in our nature to have an obsession with food. I mean, you'd die without it. Some people feel like their dying after only a couple hours. I talk about how an immigrant man made me think of all the different variety of food in the world.

How to stay home and still experience the world's finest dishes

There was a man in my yard today.

He had some kind of object with him.

It was long and big.

He turned it on. It was really loud.

But don't worry, it's just the landscaper. He comes once a week to make my yard pretty.

This man is an immigrant and as I'm driving to the gym, I can't help but think of all the foods he must enjoy in his culture.

I've asian myself but I like to experience other culture's food.

I'm particularly fond of Mexican tacos, (lengua and al pastor) the real ones, not Taco Bell.

Case in point:

Eating the same thing gets BOOOOORING.

You're a human. And humans need variety or we go bonkers.

Try this:

[Link]

Albert Noguera

Conclusion

Congratulations!

You made it to the end of the book.

That makes you weird.

Why?

According to the American Booksellers Association: 80% of Americans didn't buy or read a book this year.

But worry not, young Skywalker, the fact that you made it this far means that you're serious about success and achieving your goals.

Or you just skipped to the end.

Either way, I want to thank you for taking the time to read my book.

I've gone over the various ways to create a headline and mixing and matching them to create new ones.

Now, you've got to practice. Take immediate action on what you've learned.

Some people have taken this information and doubled their business! Some have even grew by 3x and 4x!

Make no mistake, there's gold in them hills. This book is them hills.

I'll leave you with this:

Ladies and gentlemen, there is a bible of success and the number one commandment is...

...ACTION!

This will only take 30 seconds

HELP NEEDED: Do you want me to work with you one-on-one in your business to help you double, triple or even quadruple your revenue over the next 12 months?

If yes, first you should know that I'm very expensive. My "fee" is $3,500 a month...but if you really think about it, **it really doesn't "cost" you anything.**

Because I expect to <u>make you much more than $3,500 in the first month.</u>

But I can't help everybody. I can only help businesses that meet a certain criteria. If you meet that criteria, we can proceed.

Go here, fill out the form, and once you're approved, you'll be sent an email to schedule a meeting with me.

Takes like 30 seconds...

http://albertnoguera.com/apply

Visit my website for more information on email, copywriting, and marketing strategies.

www.albertnoguera.com